SERENI-TEA

A 30-Day Devotional

Finding God's Peace
in a World of Chaos

By

Cindy Lou

The Lord bless you and keep you,

the Lord make His face shine upon you and be gracious to you.

(the Lord smile on you and gift you)

The Lord lift His countenance upon you.

(God turn His face upon you) (God looks you full in the face)

And give you PEACE.

Numbers 6:24-26

Dedications:

This book is dedicated to my Mama for always being a source of calm for me. Also, my children and grandchildren, you are all the beat of my heart. My husband for putting up with me, God bless him.

Acknowledgments:

I would like to acknowledge those that have encouraged me to live out my dream, making it a goal, to become a reality. "My special girl", Crystal Wolfe, without you this book would still be a dream. I love you. Bob Santos for his informative class, Jackie Greene for encouraging and pushing me to set goals, and Valerie Brown for being my #1 beta reader with so much insight and knowledge. My deepest appreciation to you all and the many others who have encouraged me along the process.

About the Author:

Cindy Lou lives on her homestead in Western Pennsylvania with her husband, Ralph. She is a mom of 3 adult sons and 2 adult stepdaughters, and Gammy to 13 grandchildren. She is a country girl at heart with a love of God, family, and country. Cindy has always had a passion for reading and always wanted to write a book. As a semi-retired LPN, she felt God telling her it was time. Like everyone else, she has a story and has been through much trauma and grief in her life. She writes from her heart, and her prayer is that God is glorified in her writing and that people are inspired and encouraged.

Contents

Day One

"Make every effort to live in peace with all people.
Without holiness, no one will see the Lord."
Hebrews 12:14 GW

Brothers can be the best of friends and the worst of enemies. As the mother of three boys, I had to learn to be a peacemaker. 'You boys need to learn to get along with one another!' I repeated that sentence multiple times over the years.

One thing I did to put an end to the bickering was to have the two that were fighting stand in the middle of the living room, staring into each other's eyes while holding hands. It usually didn't take very long before they were laughing and forgot what they were even fighting about. I then had them apologize, say I love you, and hug before they could run off and play again.

Living at peace with the people in our life circles-family, friends, neighbors, job, church, and groups, can take quite a bit of effort. It can be frustrating at best, sometimes. We don't get along all the time. As the saying goes, "you can't please 100% of the people 100% of the time."

So, we need to learn how to live in peace. Sometimes it is a matter of biting your tongue. Sometimes it is a matter of finding a compromise. Other times, you may need to just walk away. It doesn't mean you have to like someone, but you do have to get along.

It takes more strength and character to be at peace with someone than it does to strive against each other. As such, maintaining peace in our relationships can take some hard work. We will have to exert our peace muscles by exercising for harmony rather than strife.

Personal Reflection: *Are you living in harmony with those around you? What can you do to bring peace?*

_____

_____

_____

_____

_____

_____

_____

_____

_____

_____

_____

Day Two

"People who want to live a full life and enjoy good days must keep their tongues from saying evil things, and their lips from speaking deceitful things. They must turn away from evil and do good. They must seek peace and pursue it."

1 Peter 3:10-11 GW

One recent July fourth, we had a family reunion at our homestead. Three of our adult children and eleven of the grandchildren, ranging in age from three to thirteen, were in attendance. I had a variety of games and activities to keep them entertained all day, including a treasure hunt. I gave them clues to follow that would lead them to the "treasure chest". They knew they had found it when they looked down into the wishing well and found a white container with a big red X on it. (X marks the spot!) Their excited faces were priceless. They were enjoying a good day.

Think of the Bible as our treasure map for life. We must follow the *Scripture*s to find the treasure. (Isn't it ironic that the Bible is also our "treasure chest"?) I think God enjoys the excitement on our faces when we find a jewel in that chest and come to the understanding of peace in Him. We are to enjoy life to the fullest in Him; to do that, we should seek peace.

Isn't peace worth having to enjoy our days on this earth? Keep deceit from your lips and cultivate peace around you. Fellowship with God's people. Be a seeker in the Word, pray, and sing. These are all ways to have good days and a full life.

Personal Reflection: *Are you treasure-seeking peace? How will you pursue peace to have a joyful life?*

_____

_____

_____

_____

_____

_____

_____

_____

_____

_____

_____

_____

_____

_____

_____

_____

Day Three

"I told you all these things so that you can have peace in Me. In this world, you will have trouble, but be brave! I have defeated the world."

John 16:33 MSG

Did you know that John Wayne did not like horses? In fact, he was afraid of them. But he had a quote, "Having courage is being afraid and saddling up anyway".

Today's idiom (bumper sticker saying) is, "Do it afraid". That is what bravery is. Stepping out in faith, doing it afraid.

Jesus said that by trusting in Him, we will be unshakeable and deeply at peace (secure). He also told us that we will have difficulties in this world, but to be encouraged and brave!

Why? Because He has won the battle! He defeated death!

So, when we do have trials and troubles, and we will, we can also have peace. Jesus makes us stand firm, like an oak tree. We may bend, but we won't break. Our peace is found in Him. Matthew 10:28 tells us to not fear the man who can kill the body but not the soul. Our peace comes from knowing that we have eternal life with Jesus.

Jesus is our courage and our strength. He is strong when we are weak. Be brave and trust Jesus has your back no matter what trouble lies ahead.

Personal Reflection: Can you remember a time that you "did it afraid"? What does it mean to you to have peace in Jesus?

_____

_____

_____

_____

_____

_____

_____

_____

_____

_____

_____

_____

_____

_____

_____

Day Four

"Peace I leave with you; My peace I give you. I do not give to you as the world gives. Do not let your hearts be troubled, and do not be afraid."

John 14:27 NIV

What is peace? It seems like a simple question, but there is peace as the world gives, and there is peace as Jesus gives.

Peace, as the Oxford dictionary defines it: 1. Tranquility, freedom from disturbance; 2. A state or period in which there is no war

Synonyms of peace are calmness, restfulness, quiet, serenity, heartsease, composure, harmonious, smooth, steady, untroubled, still, free from strife, mellow, and undisturbed.

But there isn't anything or anybody that can give peace as Jesus gives it. He gave us this gift of His peace as he departed this world. His peace leaves us well and whole; not feeling abandoned, alone, and bereft as the world's peace can make us feel.

He told us not to be upset, distraught, or afraid. His peace leaves a calm feeling that all is well and good. This calmness can have a ripple effect like a pebble thrown into the water, rippling out into all the other areas of our lives.

When we have the peace Jesus gives us, we know He is with us no matter what, and all will be well.

Yesterday is over. Tomorrow may never come. Today is the present. That's why we call it a gift. Untie the ribbons and release the peace, joy, and hope it can bring.

Personal reflection: How do I feel Jesus' peace? What am I allowing to trouble my heart and keep from the gift of Jesus' peace?

_____

_____

_____

_____

_____

_____

_____

_____

_____

_____

_____

_____

_____

_____

_____

Day Five

"When I go to bed, I sleep in peace because Lord, You keep me safe."

Psalms 4:8 ERV

Now I lay me down to sleep, I pray the Lord my soul to keep. His love keeps me through the night and wakes me with the morning light. Joseph Addison

As a child, this prayer or a similar one may have been part of your bedtime routine. We have all manner of routines, doing the same things at the same times on a regular basis. Habits and schedules. We tend not to like it when we are thrown out of our routine because nothing seems to go right then or be in sync. Everything is off balance and just doesn't feel right.

We like routines because they give us a sense of security. The routine says everything is okay. Routine says we are safe; we can relax. Everything is running smoothly.

Do you have an established bedtime routine now as an adult? If not, and you are not sleeping well, maybe now is the time to make one.

We sleep better and in peace when we feel safe. An established nightly routine calms our body and readies it for sleep.

Trust God has everything in control at the day's end. Will we still have problems and situations to deal with tomorrow? Absolutely! But when we sleep in peace, we are refreshed and strengthened, ready again to take on a new day.

Personal Reflection: *Are you sleeping in peace? How can you change your nightly routine to sleep in peace?*

_____

_____

_____

_____

_____

_____

_____

_____

_____

_____

_____

_____

_____

_____

_____

_____

_____

Day Six

"Let goodness be plentiful, and righteousness burst into blossom while He lives. Let peace abound as long as there is a moon."

Psalms 72:7 GW

What is your favorite season? I enjoy summertime the most. I relish being able to sit outside on the deck swing in the mornings with a cup of coffee, just enjoying the day quietly awakening. A cool breeze blowing on a hot day. Hearing the gentle, soothing sound of cicadas lulls me to sleep at night. Visiting with family, going swimming, and having picnics.

Springtime though, is like a sigh of relief from a long Winter for the soul, giving us a much-needed lift. It fills us with encouragement. The sun shining down and warming the ground for crocuses to poke through the melting snow also regenerates our energy. We know warmer days are coming.

Apple trees begin to show off their fresh pink blossoms. Daffodils wave in the sunny breeze. Baby bunnies play tag in greening grass.

All these signs of Spring are reminders of Jesus' resurrection and the peace we have in knowing we have a new life in Him. A fresh beginning with the promise of a new life. A do-over moving forward.

When we are filled with goodness, our righteousness will come forth as fresh new blossoms as long as we live, and peace will last forever.

Personal reflection: How can my goodness be plentiful? What am I doing to bring my righteousness forth as new blossoms?

_____

_____

_____

_____

_____

_____

_____

_____

_____

_____

_____

_____

Day Seven

God says, "Be still and know that I am God; I will be exalted
among nations. I will be exalted in the earth."

Psalms 46:10 NIV

By telling us to "be still", God is telling us to stop everything we are doing. Stop moving. Stop worrying. Stop trying to fix situations. Stop thinking. Stop listening to the noise around you.

With a camera, if the subject is moving, the lens cannot focus, and the picture will be blurred and distorted. Depending on how the aperture is set, the background can be what is in focus and the subject blurred, or the subject will be clear, and the background blurred.

So it is with our inner vision. The situation can become blurred and distorted if we don't have our focus set correctly. We don't have a complete understanding, and without this, we cannot have peace. We need to be still and seek God to find that inner sense of calm that brings the situation into focus.

Peacefulness comes in quiet times of reflection or gratitude. It is your inner person getting very quiet, still, and looking to God for clarity and understanding. In critical times of stress and chaos, we need to take a moment- a time out to breathe, be still, and readjust our focus on God and not the background noise.

Worship Him and know that He is in control.

Personal Reflection: *Were you ever "out of focus" and made a poor decision? Do you remember a time that you needed to readjust your focus?*

_____

_____

_____

_____

_____

_____

_____

_____

_____

_____

_____

_____

_____

_____

_____

_____

Day Eight

"Let the peace of Christ rule in your hearts, since as members of one body you were called to peace. And be thankful."

Colossians 3:15 GW

Within any one of our life circles, such as family, church, or work, we need to get along with the others in the group to accomplish anything.

This doesn't mean we have to like everybody, but we do need to respect one another and work together, as one, like a fine-tuned machine. An organization would never be very productive or get anything done if each member took their ideas and acted upon them, it would be chaos!

Think of your life as an orchestra. Each musician learns the music for his or her instrument, but they are all playing the same symphony when they come together. They must be able to play in harmony with one another.

To do this, they have to follow their conductor. They do not play their piece or stop playing until he signals them to do so.

So too, with Christ as our conductor, we must learn to follow His instructions. We learn how to do this by reading the Bible, praying, and gathering with other Christians.

By keeping Christ as our leader, we can have His peace in our hearts and work "in tune" with one another, making beautiful music for the furtherment of the kingdom.

Personal Reflection: Are you playing solo? What can you change in your life to be in tune with others?

_____

_____

_____

_____

_____

_____

_____

_____

_____

_____

_____

_____

_____

_____

_____

Day Nine

He said, "Daniel, don't be afraid. God loves you very much.
Peace be with you. Be strong now, be courageous."

Daniel 10:19 MSG

Courage implies firmness of mind and will in the face of danger or extreme difficulty. It is the quality of mind or spirit that enables one to face danger, fear, or vicissitudes (changes) with self-possession, confidence, and resolution.

Daniel was a young man whose life sure did change! The Persian empire had invaded Israel, captured the young men, and taken them to Babylon to become slaves. How terrifying it must have been to be removed against your will from your home and taken to a strange, faraway land to become enslaved. Talk about culture shock! A foreign land, culture, and customs you didn't know, a new language to learn. And on top of that, being told you cannot worship your God.

I am sure Daniel had to be afraid. Maybe that is why the angel came to him. To comfort and strengthen him to stand firm in his belief in God. The angel assured him that everything was going to be okay. Stay calm. Take courage. Be strong. It's okay to be afraid. Be strong now; be courageous. Peace be with you. God loves you.

We can have that same peace that Daniel had. Knowing that God loves us, and He will give us the strength to do what we need to do.

Personal Reflection: What changes in your life have made you afraid? How did God bring you through it?

_____

_____

_____

_____

_____

_____

_____

_____

_____

_____

_____

_____

_____

_____

_____

Day Ten

"Now may the Lord of peace himself give/grant you His peace at all times and in every way. The Lord be with all of you."

2 Thessalonians 3:16 NIV

Some days, on my way to or from work, I will randomly call my children just to say I love them and wish them a good day. But wouldn't it be better if I said, "I love you; may God bless your day"?

How often do we bestow good wishes on our family and friends? Have a good day! Feel better soon. Thinking of you through the loss of your loved one. Greetings for a holiday or birthday. Caution them to be careful on the drive home? But what if, instead, we prayed and asked Jesus to grant them His peace?

Paul, the apostle, closed each letter with a prayer of blessing over the believers reading and hearing his words. Not just well wishes, but a prayer of blessing!

What a gift Paul bestowed on the believers at Thessalonica! A prayer for Jesus to grant His peace to them! The key phrases in this verse are "at all times" and "in every way".

At all times, this is a key phrase because it means every minute of every hour of every day. The good times and the bad, celebrations along with sorrowful times. At all times.

In every way. Whatever the situation or circumstance, whatever we are going through, He grants us peace as He meets our needs, whether Spiritual, physical, emotional, relational, or financial.

Personal Reflection: Can you think of a time in your life when someone blessed you? How can you change the way you wish people well?

_____

_____

_____

_____

_____

_____

_____

_____

_____

_____

_____

_____

_____

_____

Day Eleven

What of the wisdom from above? First, it is pure, and then peaceful, gentle, obedient, filled with mercy and good actions, fair and genuine. those who make peace sow the seeds of justice by their peaceful acts.

James 3:17-18 CEB

Wisdom is defined as the ability to do the right thing, at the right time, for the right reason.

The benefits of peace are as follows:

1.   Peace calms the storms within our spirits. Our inner conflicts. When we allow Jesus in; all is calm and peaceful.

2.   Peace takes away the heavy load of emotional baggage we carry. The baggage of regrets, shame, and disgrace, just to name a few. Peace with God ends these burdens. We can drop them at the foot of the cross and connect with the sin-bearer, Jesus. We have peace that we will never have to lift this heavy load again.

3. Peace is a chain breaker. Never again are we enslaved to sin. Never again are we held prisoner by the "old man". We are a new creation, free in God's peace.

4. Peace is our strengthening for spiritual warfare. We can stand strong, be unafraid, and be ready for battle.

5. Peace fills us with hope.

6. Peace is the basis of joy in the trials of life. We are not joyful because of the trials. We are joyful because peace with God is our uppermost solace when life throws less-than-desirable circumstances at us.

Personal Reflection: *Are you practicing peace? Do you feel your wisdom is from God?*

_____

_____

_____

_____

_____

_____

_____

_____

_____

_____

_____

_____

_____

_____

_____

Day Twelve

"For the kingdom of God is not a matter of eating and drinking.
The important things are living right with God, peace, and joy
in the Holy Spirit."

Romans 14:17 GW

There is an old saying my mom uses. Some people eat to live, and other people live to eat. She, by the way, is one of the latter. My mama just simply enjoys good food. It is a matter of where priorities lie.

A teacher once brought a jar to class and used it to teach a lesson about priorities. He filled the jar with big rocks and asked his students if the jar was full. The students replied that it was. The teacher then added small pebbles to fill the spaces between the rocks. Again, he asked the students if the jar was full, and again they agreed it was. However, the teacher added a bowl of sand, filling in all the nooks and crannies. The students once again agreed that the jar was now full. But to their surprise, the teacher then added a pitcher of water and filled the jar completely. This demonstrated that when you have the right priorities in life, you can always make room for the less important things. The jar represents your life. The rocks, pebbles, sand, and water represent all the elements in your life. The rocks are the most important things: God, family, relationships, health, and goals. The pebbles are the smaller things that matter but are not totally important: your job, home, and possessions. The sand is the little things that can fill our days, and the water is the trivial stuff that can take up our time and are really not important at all.

If you fill the jar with the unimportant things first, there is no room for the important things. When you say yes to the unimportant things, you are saying no to the important things.

What Paul is telling us in this verse is that the kingdom of God is not what you put in your stomach. (people were coming to the church just to eat) God has a different set of priorities. His priorities have to do with our lives as He sets them right and completes them with joy and peace.

Personal Reflection: *Do you need to adjust your priorities? What, in the end, will bring you more joy?*

_____

_____

_____

_____

_____

_____

_____

_____

Day Thirteen

"The fruit of that righteousness will be peace; its effect will be
quietness and confidence forever."

Isaiah 32:17 CEB

When I read this *Scripture* for the first time, my first thought was, "what righteousness?" After some research, I found the answer is God's justice. Then I asked myself, "What is God's justice?" The answer simply stated is: God's justice says that people should be treated equally and fairly because we are all made in His image.

Isaiah was looking into the future, to the coming of God's justice.

The fruit of God's righteousness or justice is peace. This peace was accomplished through Jesus' work on the cross.

By believing in Jesus, we have peace. We know that whatever heartaches this life brings, we have the confidence that we will one day be with the Savior. The progeny of peace is that we will live quiet lives and have endless trust. There is no discord within the soul. This is such a great blessing! It is a perfect peace where harmony reigns within. There is no room for jealousy, uncontrolled temper, pride, or selfishness because our heart is filled with God's perfect peace. With Jesus, we have been restored to God!

Personal Reflection: *Are you living a quiet life? What heartaches have you allowed to steal your peace?*

_____

_____

_____

_____

_____

_____

_____

_____

_____

_____

_____

_____

_____

_____

_____

_____

Day Fourteen

"How beautiful on the mountains are the feet of the messenger bringing good news, who proclaim peace, who bring good tidings, announcing salvation, who say to Zion, "Your God reigns!"

Isaiah 52:7 NIV

When someone brings you good news, they can become the most beautiful thing you have ever seen. You are so overjoyed and grateful. No longer fretting, worried, or scared within yourself. No longer wondering when, what, how, or why. The good news brings peace of mind.

This is how I felt when I got news concerning my daughter-in-law and the last set of twins she was carrying. Never have I felt so thankful in my life. Reduced to weeping and worshiping Jesus through tears of happiness and relief.

Good news helps solidify our faith that God hears and answers our prayers. Big prayers, little prayers, children's prayers, all diversity of peoples' prayers, God hears every one of them.

This was the case when the angels brought the Good News to the shepherds in the fields the night Jesus was born. The shepherds then related the Good News to everyone they encountered. It was the news the Jewish people had been praying for and waiting for centuries to hear! Emmanuel! God with us!

God's plan was going forth with the proclamation of the Good News: Our God reigns!

Have peace today, knowing that God is with you; this is very good news!

Personal Reflection: *What good news have you been waiting for? What good news can you share with others to give them peace?*

_____

_____

_____

_____

_____

_____

_____

_____

_____

_____

_____

_____

_____

_____

_____

_____

Day Fifteen

"But He was pierced for our transgressions, He was crushed for our iniquities; the punishment that brought us peace was on Him, and by His wounds, we are healed."

Isaiah 53:5 NIV

When we do something wrong or bad, there is usually a punishment when it is discovered. Some of the scariest words my mom could say to me were "Wait until your father gets home!" This struck fear in me because I knew I had done wrong, was in trouble, and most likely would get a spanking.

But have you taken the blame and punishment for something you did not do?

In the Old Testament, once a year, the priest would take a goat and lay the sins of the nation on its head to carry them away. The goat would then be led out of the city, led into the wilderness, and left to wander. It received the punishment the people deserved. This was called a scapegoat.

Jesus was our scapegoat. He took upon himself all the sins of mankind and withstood the punishment of the cross, which we so richly deserve.

Our peace knowing this is that if we believe in Jesus and accept Him as our Savior, we will never be separated from God. There will be no enmity between us. We will not be sent out into the wilderness to roam aimlessly lost. We will be the found sheep. We will be the "one". We will be safe in the Shepherd's arms. This is the gift of God's merciful love.

Personal Reflection: *Did you ever take the punishment for something you didn't do? How did it make you feel?*

_____

_____

_____

_____

_____

_____

_____

_____

_____

_____

_____

_____

_____

_____

_____

Day Sixteen

"With perfect peace, You will protect those whose minds cannot
be changed, because they trust You."

Isaiah 26:3   GW

True peace is all-encompassing. It covers and protects everything. It is dependable.

You could illustrate it as an oversized quilt on a winter night. Wrapped up and snuggling by the fireplace. The quilt covers you completely and protects you from the cold. You could say it is all-encompassing.

When it is freezing outside, you depend on that quilt to protect you. You trust it will keep you warm. You have peace of mind that you won't be cold and shivering. Now with a steaming cup of hot chocolate and just the right ratio of marshmallows, it's downright cozy watching the snow come down while you're all nice and toasty in your quilt.

It is the same way in trusting God. We have true peace as we depend on Him because we know we can trust Him to cover us completely. He shields and protects us as we rest under His wings.

God cares about every tiny detail in every area of our lives. So even though it may be storming outside, we are quiet and whole inside.

Personal Reflection: Do you trust God with each aspect of your life? How has God's peace covered you?

_____

_____

_____

_____

_____

_____

_____

_____

_____

_____

_____

_____

_____

Day Seventeen

"For to us a Child is born, to us, a Son is given, and the government will be on His shoulders. And He will be called Wonderful Counselor, Mighty God, Everlasting Father, Prince of Peace."

Isaiah 9:6 NIV

Do you remember reading Little Golden Books as a child? Maybe you are reading them to your child now. One book in particular I enjoyed is called, "The House That Jack Built."

It is a rhyming book written in *syntactic structure*, meaning each sentence in the story is an example of an increasingly deeply nested relative cause. It is a cumulative story that doesn't even tell the story of Jack's house or even Jack; but it shows how the house is indirectly related to other things and people, showing how all these smaller events are interlinked.

Psychologists are using these types of cumulative stories to calm anxiousness. Interesting fact considering having Jesus means having peace.

We could think of the birth of Jesus, our Prince of Peace, in a syntactic form. Jesus is our Prince of Peace. Peace is wholeness. Wholeness is completeness. Completeness is perfection. We are perfect in Jesus. We are complete in Jesus. We are whole in Jesus. We are at peace in Jesus. All of this is interconnected because of the birth of Jesus.

Personal Reflection: *How am I perfect in Jesus? Is Jesus my Prince of Peace, and how?*

_____

_____

_____

_____

_____

_____

_____

_____

_____

_____

_____

_____

_____

_____

_____

_____

_____

Day Eighteen

'Wisdom's ways are pleasant ways, and all its paths lead to peace.'

Proverbs 3:17 GW

Wisdom is likened to a lady in the book of Proverbs, depicting her manner as beautiful and, her ways as pleasant. Lady Wisdom's life is wonderfully complete and whole; her pathways are of peace.

Have you ever been told, "If you would just listen to me?"

Someone more experienced and educated than you is trying to teach you how to do something, but you want to do it your way. You want to figure it out on your own.

Why do we, as human beings, always have to be stubborn about choosing wisely? If we would just listen to those who have experience, if we would just listen to wisdom, life would be so much easier and happier.

It seems to take many of us years to mature and realize this. We need to learn from whom wisdom comes *If any of you lacks wisdom, you should ask God. James 1:5*

In other words, pray about every decision you have to make. Seek God's will and plan. He will make straight your paths.

Making good choices makes us wise. Make a choice to listen to people who have wisdom. Choose your friends wisely.

Turn neither to the right nor to the left but turn your foot from evil.
Proverbs 4:27.

Stay on the straight and narrow path of wisdom. For it makes life peaceful. And a peaceful life is a pleasant life.

Personal Reflection: *What wise choice have you made lately? Do you pray about decisions before making them?*

_____

_____

_____

_____

_____

_____

_____

_____

_____

_____

_____

_____

_____

_____

_____

_____

.

Day Nineteen

"Deceit is in the hearts of those who plot evil, but those who promote peace have joy."

Proverbs 12:20 NIV

I like to make jelly during the summer months. Each month a different type of berry is in season. There are strawberries in June, black raspberries in July, quickly followed by blackberries, and lastly, in late August or early September, there are elderberries.

I use the same recipes each year. They take different amounts of juice and sugar, but the one thing that is the same in all of them is the instructions to stir constantly until a rolling boil cannot be stirred down. Why? It's so the liquid doesn't rest and scorch to the bottom of the pan. You have to keep it agitated and stirred up.

There are people in this world who like to cause drama and unrest, keeping things agitated and stirred up. They like to spread gossip. I tend to call these people "pot stirrers". They like to get all the information they can on people and then repeat it to cause strife, aka drama. They may even embellish the gossip, making it more enticing and apt to be spread further. These are the kind of people that the book of Proverbs warns us to avoid and not to do as they do.

We are instead, to be peacemakers. Not drama llamas. Let the gossip stop at your door. Don't listen to it, and don't repeat it. Stand up for peace. You will be happy and make others happy too.

Personal Reflection: *Do I behave like a pot-stirrer or a peacemaker? How can I plan peace?*

_____

_____

_____

_____

_____

_____

_____

_____

_____

_____

_____

_____

_____

_____

_____

_____

Day Twenty

"By faith, we have been made acceptable to God. And now, thanks to our Lord Jesus Christ, we have peace with God."

Romans 5:1 CEV

Many in this world need to see something to believe in it. Seeing is believing. But faith is defined as a trust or belief in a person or thing without proof.

Some may ask, "Have you ever seen God?"

"No, but I have seen the evidence of His existence and goodness." I ask, "Can you see the wind? No, but you can see evidence of its existence and power."

When we come to believe in God and accept Jesus as our Savior and Lord, we are made right with Him. Which means we are in the right standing with God. We can have a relationship with Him. A peaceful relationship because Jesus has taken our sins on Himself so that we are no longer at enmity with Him.

This relationship needs work, just as any other relationship we have. We talk and pray with God. We read His Word to know his heart. We worship and give thanks. We are not bound by legalism but by our love for Him.

When trials come, people may feel that God is testing them or punishing them. We need to understand that we live in a fallen world. Many of our problems are self-inflicted by making poor choices.

Let us understand that God is the one who stands with us in the fire. When we trust Him, we are being refined, strengthening our faith, and we will have peace with God.

Personal Reflection: In what ways can I strengthen my relationship with God? How will this give me peace with him?

_____

_____

_____

_____

_____

_____

_____

_____

_____

_____

_____

_____

_____

_____

Day Twenty-one

"If our minds are ruled by our desires, we will die. But if our minds are ruled by the Spirit, we will have life and peace."

Romans 8:6 CEV

Have you ever had to have plumbing replaced at your house and thought, "I can do this myself," instead of calling an expert plumber? In a sitcom, it is a humorous storyline. But in real life, it can turn into a costly disaster.

People who live self-centered lives have a DIY life. They don't rely on the expert. They either don't know they need God, or they think that they don't need God. But trying to *Do It Yourself* only leads to more problems.

They focus only on themselves and what they want or what they think they need to make them happy: money, big homes, popularity, or fancy cars. Material things. They believe they can accomplish this all on their own. They chase after "happy" only to have "happy" move when they get it because it doesn't satisfy them. They live a dead life.

They fail to realize that they are in bondage. They are slaves to their desires. They work harder and harder to have the life they think they want.

But people who live alongside the Spirit have what the Spirit desires in mind. They want what He wants. They live a life of freedom and peace because they have been delivered from that dead life. They are happy and content.

This doesn't mean we will never have problems. The plumbing still goes bad and needs replacing. But you can be assured that there is nothing in that old Do it Yourself life for you. Leave it behind and follow God where He leads, after all, He is the Expert!

Personal Reflection: Are you living a DIY life? Are you willing to follow God where he leads and give Him control?

_____

_____

_____

_____

_____

_____

_____

_____

_____

_____

_____

_____

_____

_____

_____

Day Twenty-two

"… and the peace of God, which transcends all understanding,
will guard your hearts and minds through Jesus Christ."

Philippians 4:7   NIV

I don't understand how the internet works. But I know I can video chat with my family. I know I can look up any trivia question and have an answer within seconds. I know it has clouds that store my files. How? I don't know. I just know I tap some keys, and it works.

As I read this *Scripture* many thoughts quickly went through my mind. There must be 100 or more sermons that could be preached from this verse. How does the peace of God guard your heart and mind? Why do our hearts and minds need to be protected by the peace of God? How tiny our minds must be that we cannot comprehend the peace of God. How great the peace of God must be that we cannot understand it. I have no understanding of these questions.

But these things I am sure of: I don't need to understand the peace of God to have it and feel it. I just need to have faith in it. I don't need to know how it protects my heart and mind; I just need to believe it does.

Then when trials come, and my mind creates false narratives causing fear and anxiety, all I need to know and believe is that by trusting God, His peace will keep my heart from failing. His peace, through Jesus Christ, will protect my spirit.

Personal Reflection: How has the peace of God protected your heart in the past? How can Jesus protect your spirit in the future?

_____

_____

_____

_____

_____

_____

_____

_____

_____

_____

_____

_____

_____

_____

_____

_____

_____

Day Twenty-three

"When a man's ways please the Lord, He makes even his enemies
to be at peace with him." Proverbs 16:7 NKJ

Romans 12:20 says: *if your enemy is thirsty, give him a drink, if he is*
hungry, feed him, by doing so, you heap hot coals on his head.

Have you ever been bullied or made fun of? When I was in grade
school, there was a boy on the bus that picked on me every single day.
He called me "Jap eyes". Now I had no idea what he meant by it, but I
knew how it made me feel.

But as a lot of mothers would, my mom told me to ignore him.
Yet sometimes it just wasn't that easy. I seemed to have a target on my
back. How could I ignore and be kind to those who tormented me?
However, this is also how God wants us to behave. This displays a
positive Christian attitude.

Does this mean that we should not stand up for ourselves?
Certainly not. We need to stand firm in our beliefs, but there are more
positive Christian attributes to utilize than retaliation.

You have heard the saying: you can catch more flies with honey than you can with vinegar. You are to be kind to the person who is unkind to you. Compliment those who insult you. Praise those that belittle you; pray for those that persecute you.

This verse comes with a promise. It says when we live to please God, we will have peace with the thorn in our side because they will make peace with us.

Personal Reflection: *Who is a thorn in my side that I cannot seem to make peace with? Do I pray for that person; am I kind to them?*

_____

_____

_____

_____

_____

_____

_____

_____

_____

_____

_____

_____

_____

_____

Day Twenty-four

"Finally, brothers and sisters, rejoice! Strive for full restoration, encourage one another, be of one mind; live in peace. And the God of love and peace will be with you."

2 Corinthians 13:11 NIV

It doesn't seem to matter what group you are involved in: whether at work, school, club, or church, when there is a project to do, everyone agrees it should be done. A discussion takes place as to how it should be done and when. But when the time comes to participate, not everyone shows up.

Paul tells us in his farewell letter to church members in Corinth, to strive for peace within the church. To be in harmony with one another. One way to do this is to encourage one another in the sharing of their gifts.

Is it possible some don't "do" in the church because they have never been encouraged to? Has anyone ever personally asked them what they could do to help with a project or activity? Have they been asked if they would like to participate?

Maybe someone is not comfortable teaching Sunday School but is able to financially provide the materials. Is there another who is unable to lead the worship music but could lead the congregational prayer? Possibly someone has a mower but not the time; he could lend the mower to someone who has the time, and someone else provides the gas. While somebody cleans the floors, another cleans the pews. There is something everyone can do, and they should be given the opportunity to do it.

When everyone comes together and gives what they have to offer, we can work together to maintain peace. Every aspect of your group's activities and duties should be discussed and agreed upon to have one accord.

Personal Reflection: Do I encourage people to participate? What can I do to encourage participation?

_____

_____

_____

_____

_____

_____

_____

_____

_____

_____

_____

_____

_____

Day Twenty-five

"When we worship the right way, God doesn't stir us up into confusion; He brings us into harmony (peace). This goes for all the churches-no exceptions."

1 Corinthians 14:33 MSG

If you have ever played a sport, you know there is no "I" in "team". Everyone has to come together under the coach's leadership. Each team member may have his own position and job to do, but working for the same end result makes the team run like a well-oiled machine. If each team member tried to be the leader or do everything on his own or only what he wanted to do, there would be chaos and a definite loss.

It is the same in a church. There is a format or routine that is followed. Usually, a board of directors sets up the bylaws of the church and also how the church service will be conducted. The pastor is under the board but leads the parishioners in worshiping and serving God.

Because not everyone can be a pastor or Sunday School teacher, each member has a different job to do in the church. Whether it is as a pianist, worship leader, sound person, or prayer warrior, all must work together for the furtherment of the kingdom.

This is worshiping the right way. When each one does his part in an organized and peaceful manner it unifies the church, and worship to God is performed together as a team.

Personal Reflection: Do I behave like there is an "I" in team? In what ways do I worship God?

_____

_____

_____

_____

_____

_____

_____

_____

_____

_____

_____

_____

_____

_____

_____

_____

_____

Day Twenty-six

"Those who love your teachings will find true peace, and nothing will defeat them."

Psalms 119:165 NKJV

Everyone who knows me knows my favorite holiday is Christmas. I enjoy absolutely everything that goes with it. The shopping, decorations, lights, cookies, gifts, trees, and the loving Spirit of the season.

But I especially enjoy the music. If I could only ever listen to one genre of music for the rest of my life, it would be Christmas music. It tells The Story of the miraculous birth of the Messiah. Brought to reconcile God and man. It elicits happiness and feelings of joy. It encourages and gives hope. It puts into words all my emotions and thoughts about each person involved in this wondrous event.

Spoiler alert: if you ride in my car with me, my Christmas music starts the day after Thanksgiving and goes until January 7th.

Today's verse reminds me of a Christmas song recorded by Randy Travis: *"Nothin's Gonna Bring Me Down (at Christmas Time)"*. It's about a guy who is really having a tough time. The water pipes are frozen, he has no money, the car battery is dead, and everything that could go wrong did go wrong.

The encouraging thing about it, though, is his attitude through it all. Even though all these seemingly hard times come upon him, he stays positive. He says, "I'm gonna be just fine; nothin's gonna bring me down at Christmas time." Just the sheer joy of the season keeps his spirit high.

This is what it is like for the man who loves God's teachings and puts them into practice. He has learned to trust God and His plan and His provision. He has found true peace, and nothing will defeat him.

Personal Reflection: *What have you let cause you to feel defeated in the past? Do you feel you now have true peace? Why or why not?*

_____

_____

_____

_____

_____

_____

_____

_____

_____

_____

_____

_____

_____

_____

Day Twenty-seven

"The mountains may move, and the hills may shake, but My kindness will never depart from you. My promise of peace will never change," says the Lord who has compassion on you."

Isaiah 54:10 GW

"Can we have a fairy garden every year, Gammy?" asked three of my granddaughters who were vacationing with my husband and me on our farm. "Of course, pinkie promise!", I exclaim, while holding out my smallest finger. "What's a pinkie promise?", they asked with quizzical looks on their faces. I explained that when you make a vow or promise and want to assure the other person that you won't break that promise, you hook your pinkie fingers and shake. This makes it a solid promise. So, we made our pinkie promise, and each summer they come to visit, the very first thing they say is, "We have to build the fairy garden!"

They look forward to placing all the houses, accessories, and fairies and then receiving letters and little gifts from the "fairies". It is such a treasure of memories for all of us.

But these days, it seems people treat promises like they are just words with no meaning or value. Promises are never meant to be broken or taken lightly. They are more than mere words. When you add, "I promise", to a statement, it is more powerful because if the promise is broken, so is trust. And trust cannot easily be restored.

People tend to get very upset when you don't keep a promise. It makes them feel like they are unimportant. It also shows you are not trustworthy; you cannot be trusted to keep your word. This can not only harm your relationship because the trust is gone, but also mar your reputation.

Thankfully, God is trustworthy. When He makes a promise, we can trust Him to keep it. His Word is full of promises. God cannot break a promise just like He cannot lie. He set his rainbow in the sky thousands of years ago as a promise, and He promises you peace now.

Personal Reflection: Do I treat promises as sacred trusts or just mere words? What promises have I made and then broken?

_____

_____

_____

_____

_____

_____

_____

_____

_____

_____

Day Twenty-eight

"Now may the God of peace himself sanctify you completely, and may your whole spirit, soul, and body be kept blameless at the coming of our Lord Jesus Christ."

1 Thessalonians 5:23 ESV

When a ship is sinking, literally or metaphorically, the crew works feverishly to stop the inflow of water while also doing everything they can to save everyone they can. But if they cannot stop the incoming water, there comes the point when the captain gives the order: "Every man for himself!" In other words, forget about saving the ship or anyone else. Do whatever you can to save yourself!

But we are talking about salvation, and the problem is we cannot save ourselves. Jesus is the only One who could have saved Himself had He given in to His will. Thankfully though, He said, "Father, Your will be done."

Jesus told His followers He is the only way to the Father. The bystanders at the cross told Jesus if He truly was the Messiah to save Himself and come down from the cross. They did not understand that He had to die to save them and us.

Through the shedding of His blood, we have remission of sin. We, therefore, are made holy through Him. We are blameless in the eyes of God because of this.

Had Jesus come down from the cross, we would be the very opposite of peaceful. We would be lost, alone, and restless. We can only come to the God of peace through Jesus. The only way to do that is through His sacrifice.

Personal Reflection: When the "ship" is sinking, do you think of others first or every man for himself? Can you think of a time when you tried to save yourself?

_____

_____

_____

_____

_____

_____

_____

_____

_____

_____

_____

_____

_____

_____

_____

Day Twenty-nine

"Grace and peace to you many times over as you deepen in your experience with God and Jesus, our Master."

2 Peter 1:2 MSG

Annie Johnston Flint lived from 1866 to 1932. She was a dear servant of Jesus. She was orphaned twice, crippled with arthritis at a young age, and had a younger sister to care for. Yet she remained convinced that God was going to glorify Himself through her weak, earthly body. She started writing greeting cards for friends. This led to her writing poetry which she gave as gifts of encouragement. Then she began selling them to have an income. Eventually, some of her poems were set to music and became hymns. "He Giveth More Grace" was one such poem. The last line of the first stanza reads: To multiplied trials, His multiplied peace.

While others seem to have an easier course to sail in life, you may feel like you are constantly treading water just to stay afloat. Sometimes you may feel as though you have a black cloud hanging over your head.

At times it seems as though your burdens are too much to bear. The waves of life on this earth continually overtake you.

So many times, we may need to adjust our thoughts. Do you look at your glass as half empty or half full? Are you a positive thinker or a negative thinker? Do you believe God is testing you or preparing you? Do you have an attitude of gratitude or one of complaining that nothing ever goes your way?

As you continue your journey with God and grow as a believer, you will have your share of valleys to walk through. But when you get to the mountain top, oh, the view! God has been exercising your faith muscles to trust Him all the more, and that trust leads to peace.

Personal Reflection: *Do I need to change my thoughts? Do I have an attitude of gratitude, and if not, what can I do to change it?*

_____

_____

_____

_____

_____

_____

_____

_____

_____

_____

_____

_____

_____

Day Thirty

"For I know the plans that I have for you, declares the Lord. They are plans of peace and not disaster, plans to give you a future filled with hope."

Jeremiah 29:11 GW

Isn't it wonderful and comforting to know that God has a plan for us? We may not know exactly what it is, but we do know that when we follow the pathway that He has uniquely laid out for each of us, we will have peace. He cares for us and wants us to have a future filled with hope living in Him.

Our whole purpose in this life is to love God with our whole being, heart, mind, and soul. Whatever career path we choose, we should do it for the Lord. Whatever hobbies we enjoy could become our ministry if we do it for God. We can make a difference when we seek and obey Him.

Whatever difficulties or trials come our way, whatever course we choose to take, His purpose will be fulfilled through us when we trust Him to do so. Even when we go astray, He can use our mistakes for

His good and perfect will. He can and will fulfill His planned purpose for us.

We make so difficult what can be so simple. But that is our human nature, to want what we want when we want it. We follow our selfish desires instead of waiting on the Lord. When we do this, we can really mess things up and get off the track the Lord wants us on. But when we live for Him and in Him, we make better choices because we want what He wants. This leads to having the peace and joy we so desire.

Personal Reflection: Do my desires align with God's plan for my life? Am I making choices based on my desires?

_____

_____

_____

_____

_____

_____

_____

_____

_____

_____

_____

_____

_____

_____

_____

_____

_____

www.ingramcontent.com/pod-product-compliance
Lightning Source LLC
Chambersburg PA
CBHW051632120626
46551CB00014B/2042